27/a

W9-BWP-569

Kentucky's Age of Wood

KENNETH CLARKE

and

IRA KOHN

THE UNIVERSITY PRESS OF KENTUCKY

Research for The Kentucky Bicentennial Bookshelf
is assisted by a grant from the
National Endowment for the Humanities.
Views expressed in the Bookshelf do not
necessarily represent those of the Endowment.

ISBN: 0-8131-0225-1

Library of Congress Catalog Card Number: 76-4432

A statewide cooperative scholarly publishing agency
serving Berea College, Centre College of Kentucky,
Eastern Kentucky University, The Filson Club,
Georgetown College, Kentucky Historical Society,
Kentucky State University, Morehead State University,
Murray State University, Northern Kentucky University,
Transylvania University, University of Kentucky,
University of Louisville, and Western Kentucky University.

Editorial and Sales Offices: Lexington, Kentucky 40506

Contents

1

BITS OF HISTORY

IN A SMALL COUNTRY STORE in Western Kentucky an observant customer can see a remarkably simple butcher's block. It now serves as a work or storage surface behind a meat display case that contains only packaged meat and dairy products. The butcher's block is a reminder of some earlier time when the store provided more services than it does now. It is also a reminder of Kentucky forests and forest products of the past. The block is simply a section of a sycamore tree trunk, supported by iron pipes driven into the bottom side for legs. More than three feet in diameter and a foot thick, the massive cylinder of solid, close-grained wood is impressive. Inquiry reveals that this and similar blocks were cut from a newly felled sycamore in Butler County only twenty years before Kentucky's bicentennial. The owner doesn't know where to find a tree of that size and symmetry now, though he recalls that there were many big trees still standing when he was younger. A bystander remarks that elm should make a good butcher's block because it is so resistant to splitting.

Just a few miles from the country store a schoolboy comes up from an arrowhead hunt along the banks of the Barren River. He is carrying two sets of rusty chain dogs, each set consisting of two small iron wedges about six inches long joined by six links of chain. The boy explains that he pried them out of logs exposed by low water. The logs buried in riverbottom mud are part of a long-lost raft. An old-timer remarks that the raft probably had lots of "sinkers" in it. Possibly it broke up in a storm or floodwaters and sank to the bottom before it could be located and recovered. It remains as a curiosity, the tops of the logs barely visible when the water level is abnormally low. A knowledgeable veteran of the woods suggests that some of the logs buried in the mud would deteriorate very little. If salvaged, the sunken raft might contain some marketable timber. The boy freely gives a set of chain dogs to a neighbor who wants them for a keepsake. There are more to be had for the taking. He is not unduly impressed by his find, for he lives surrounded by similar reminders of a way of life partly conditioned by a forest environment. Every day as he does his chores he passes an unused double-pen log house hand fashioned by his forebears. A neighbor's spacious barn conceals at its center the old log crib barn, complete with threshing floor, that first served the farmstead. Though the threshing floor is no longer used, the ancient log compartment is still a functional part of the larger structure built around and over it.

All over the state of Kentucky one encounters these homely reminders of a time when products of the great forests were more accessible than products of the foundry and factory, a time when every man knew the value of a well sharpened ax, and most men could identify the species of a tree practically as far away as they could distinguish it in the forest.

This is an account of some of the ordinary objects and tools associated with the great age of wood in Kentucky. It will for the most part omit reference to professional or journeyman work of architects, artists, and furniture makers—those whose careers are devoted to special skills and products. It will sample the traditional uses of wood by ordinary people who did not have professional training. The exceptional expression, be it a house or a song, is idiosyncratic. It calls attention to itself and its maker. Although the humble, anonymous, everyday objects are thrown into shadow by the exceptional, those humble objects may be truer reflections of the history of all Kentucky's people than the well preserved, much advertised landmark.

Everywhere in Kentucky, in old barns, attics, cellars, woodsheds—even in the sinkholes filled with rubbish—one sees bits of history. In some small degree the popularity of collecting old objects and trading them at flea markets is bringing some of these to light. Hand-carved children's toys, white-oak feed baskets, wooden carpenter's tools are sought after by the antique hunter. Some of these display a degree of workmanship that gives them an authentic aesthetic appeal. But buyers at flea markets and auctions are still passing over many wooden artifacts whose texture or shape fails to arouse admiration. Sometimes the collectors do not even "see" the objects because their uses have been forgotten.

One reason for our familiarity with excellent historical buildings and their furnishings is that they are cared for and displayed. Wood succumbs quickly to fire, insects, and decay if it is not protected. The old smokehouse, no matter how typical it is or how skillfully built, sinks quickly into oblivion when its roof is gone. The hand-crafted bull-tongue plow exposed to the elements melts away and becomes a part of the weed patch that once concealed it. Ironically, relics most representative of the period of Kentucky's history dominated by wood—the houses, barns, bridges, rafts, tools, furnishings, even the forests themselves—are less immediately apparent and certainly less publicized than the more admired and less typical products of fewer hands.

2

THE PIONEER AND HIS TOOLS

ONE REASON for the astonishingly rapid decimation of the virgin forests of Kentucky is that the pioneers who cleared the land were experienced woodsmen. For more than a century before the construction of Fort Harrod, American colonists had been perfecting their tools and techniques. The original colonists, who brought European woodworking skills to the New World, had to clear seemingly inexhaustible stands of forest to make room for cultivated fields. Coming from European settlements long deforested or containing relatively fewer and smaller species of trees, they found trees of enormous size and species in such abundance that a new age of wood technology was inevitable. Lacking the metallurgical resources of the Old World, pioneers were thrown upon their ingenuity to make do with what was available. As immigration continued, shipwrights, millwrights, carpenters, wheelwrights, coopers and other craftsmen brought together the lore and tools of their various trades from many European countries. The result was a kind of hybrid vigor, a pooling, adaptation, and selection of the most useful, whatever its origin. An eighteenth-century settler in western New York state might employ a German millwright, trade with an Irish cooper, and build his barn

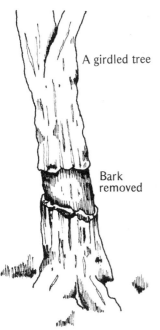

A girdled tree

Bark removed

after the design of Scandinavian log constructions. His flintlock rifle might be the product of Pennsylvania gunsmiths of German descent, but its curly maple stock would be an American specialty. Because some of the hardwood trees on his land would be too large to fell and dispose of easily, he might girdle them to kill the foliage and let the sunlight in, then plow around the enormous skeletons, deferring their disposal to a later time. There were giants in the forest in the early years, and there were giants among the axmen who set out to clear the land.

Judging by the evidence of archaeology, the ax, a chopping head fastened to a handle, is one of mankind's earliest tools. Stone ax heads made by the aboriginal Indians of Kentucky are commonly found in amateur collections of Indian artifacts. Evidence all around the world indicates that early man made much use of this basic tool. Museum collections of early American axes show that many designs were brought to this continent, some rather inefficient and not substantially different from their medieval prototypes.

The development of the ax into its several modern efficient shapes and weights is largely an American phenomenon. The frontiersman's most essential belongings were his ax and his gun. The Kentuckian's legendary marksmanship with his muzzle-loading rifle reflects a skill used much less regularly than his skill with an ax, and just as he gave particular attention to caring for his gun, so he gave particular attention to the care of his ax.

Watch a modern urban adult get wood for his campfire. He digs out a "hand" ax. It has a factory-cut handle about eighteen inches long, probably painted green. The miniature poll ax head weighs about a pound and a half. It may be painted green also, even to the bevel of the cutting edge. The camper picks out a likely looking tree about six inches in diameter and proceeds to cut it down. He has selected it for size and convenience, but he doesn't know the species. He swings mightily at the tree, barely denting its bark. He swings again and again, enlarging his dent and exhausting his energy. Because he is young, strong, healthy, and determined, he finally succeeds without precipitating a heart attack. The stump of the felled tree looks as though it has been attacked by a squad of beavers. After catching his breath, the now thoroughly aroused camper sets out to cut off a length of its trunk for his fire. By now he has the knack of chopping out a small chip at a time, and after many enlargements of the width of his cut, he produces a two-foot section of a six-inch tree. Triumphantly, he decides to split it. He props it up on end and drives a lusty blow dead center into his log. His ax sticks. He wrenches at it furiously and breaks the handle—a poor handle, machine cut across the grain. Enraged, the camper gets a hammer and drives the ax head deeper into the log to make it perform the function of a wedge. When he finally gets his green log split and recovers his battered ax head, his troubles have just begun. He will yet have to learn that he cannot make the green wood burn.

An old-timer would have a few words of advice: Get a chopping ax instead of a toy. It should have enough weight to drive deeply into the wood by its own momentum. Be sure that it is well tempered steel with a uniformly sharpened cutting edge. Better yet, have two cutting edges, a keen one for chopping, the other one for brushing and rough work. Put the efficient ax head on a well seasoned, straight-grained handle of the proper

6

length. Clear away the brush so that you can take a full, easy, accurate swing. Let the tool do the work; save your breath. Chips as big as your hand will fly out of the wide notch as you chop. The tree can be felled with a few easy strokes, but you should be sure that you have picked the right kind of tree for your intended use. A green sapling will not do for a campfire.

The old-timer would have other kinds of advice—how to split a log, why one should not pound on one metal tool with another metal tool. This is not to say that there are no modern Kentuckians who know how to work wood; it is meant to say that practical knowledge about wood and hand tools has ceased to be common property, part of the everyday knowledge of every man.

In the age of wood an almost universal rite of passage was the gift of a pocketknife to a boy as soon as he was old enough to use one. He soaked up wood lore without formal instruction from an environment in which there was no escaping the knowledge. He learned the proverbial cautions: "Never cut toward yourself," and "A dull blade is more dangerous than a sharp one." Hardly aware of how he learned, he knew as he matured that wood from a white walnut tree is easier to work than wood from a black walnut; that beech is difficult to work and warps easily; that white oak will warp more than walnut; that red oak rots at the heart much sooner than post oak; that sassafras trees big enough to make timber produce a beautiful, light, hard, workable, durable wood; and that boxelder isn't very useful on any account.

With growing interest in old tools as antiques or decorations, the broadax has become a familiar object once more. The large number of broadax heads dug out of old woodsheds, barns, and attics for trade at flea markets or for sale to antique dealers is a rough indicator of how familiar this tool has been in Kentucky's past. If a novice picks up a good broadax, feels its massive weight, sights along its crooked handle, and thumbs its chisel edge, he

7

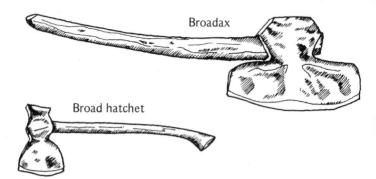

Broadax

Broad hatchet

might remark on its inadequacy as a chopping tool. He would be right. The broadax is designed for hewing instead of chopping. Even if its cutting edge were beveled on both sides to razor sharpness, it would be too heavy and awkwardly shaped to swing properly to fell a tree. Furthermore, its handle is neither the right length nor of the right configuration to permit good chopping action. No other widely used woodworking tool is so closely associated with the houses and barns built in Kentucky from the time of the first settlement until well into the twentieth century. Its function is to hew flat surfaces, to transform a log into a beam or a heavy board.

A typical broadax will have from twelve to thirteen inches of cutting edge, roughly three times as much cutting edge as a light poll ax or chopping ax. The broadax will measure from eight to nine inches from edge to poll (head), and its eye (for insertion of the handle) will bulge out on one side, leaving the other side perfectly plane so that it can work flat against the timber. The side of the blade opposite the handle is beveled to form a cutting edge, like the bevel edge on a chisel. The heads of broadaxes that turn up at flea markets and auctions are sometimes diminished in size as a result of wear. Because the tool must be keenly sharp to function properly, some of its bulk has been ground away at the grindstone. Examination of a well worn broadax in an antique store in

8

Morehead, for example, showed that it had been reduced almost two inches from its original cutting edge, thereby suffering a loss of at least two pounds of weight, with a corresponding loss of effectiveness, since the broadax is designed to hew by its own weight and inertia rather than by muscle power behind the stroke.

What appears to the novice to be a defectively crooked handle emerging from the offset eye is in reality a triumph of traditional wood craftsmanship. A straight handle would cause the worker's knuckles to knock against the timber if he tried to keep the massive blade flat against his work. To save his hands, and to decrease his temptation to tilt the point of his ax into the work, he warps the handle so that it bends away from the flat side of the ax. One veteran of the woods stated that he ordinarily chose a straight hickory tree large enough to yield a good handle billet from each half after it was split. While the billets cured, natural warping of each half would produce the desired curvature. He would then work them down with a drawknife to the shape he wanted. Then, he remarked, he would have a right-handed handle and a left-handed handle. It is true that the ax must be reversed for a change from a right-handed hewer to a left-handed hewer, but this can be accomplished in some instances by merely removing the handle as it emerges from one side and inserting it into the other. But unless the broadax head has a symmetrical eye that will permit this reversal, separate right- and left-handed handles are necessary.

Hewing a log with a broadax requires some preparation. The log must be supported on crosspieces or low horses to raise it clear of the ground, and it must be turned so that the plane surface to be produced will be vertical. This allows the workman to stand beside the log and chop straight down to smooth the flat surface he is working on. Before he begins this phase, however, he must mark the log from end to end so that he can hew to the line, and he must score the log at intervals so that he can chop away short sections instead of a cumbersome slab the length of the log. To make his mark he snaps a chalkline stretched from end to end. He then scores the log with an ordinary chopping ax by cutting vertical notches into the side of the log, chopping only as far as the chalkline mark. Ordinarily he stands on top of the log and chops down into its side to score it. Finally, with the log marked and scored, the worker stands beside it and begins to hew away the slabs with his broadax, letting the weight of the ax do most of the work as it falls. The blows will peel away slabs large enough to serve as firewood. To keep the momentum of the heavy blade from carrying it all the way into the ground, the hewer lays some of the big chips crossways under the log being worked. After his first rough pass, he works down the length of the log again, this time using deft, light strokes to smooth up the surface. The quality of the plane surface thus produced is what distinguishes the "slick hewer." A slick hewer, as one observer put it, "can split a fly down the middle."

A precise hewer may demand even more of his tool than it could produce as a perfectly plane blade from the factory. A straight cutting edge, if tilted ever so slightly, will catch its points in the work, producing gouges. To make the blade more useful for shaving away small irregularities, the slick hewer "bucked" a new blade so that the cutting edge would curve slightly at the center, cutting more there than at the tips. To buck a new ax head, the worker would place it flat on a stump and elevate each end of the cutting edge with thin wooden chips. He would then strike the center with a sharp blow of a sledgehammer to produce the desired curvature. A broadax thus modified will cut away thin shavings with the middle portion of its edge, leaving the tips free so that they will not hang up or dig into the work. One old-time logger recalls that his father lost a week's income during hard times when he broke a new ax head in two by bucking it too energetically.

Rummaging through a box of rusty old tools a collector came across the badly battered head of what appeared to be an old-fashioned hatchet. Examination showed that it was flat-sided and had a bevel on only one side of its edge. It was a broad hatchet, the diminutive version of the broadax. Somewhere in its history it has lost its handle. Unrecognized as a useful tool, it had become a wedge, and misused as a metal wedge, it had been pounded with a heavy metal hammer. It is illustrated on page 8 equipped (improperly) with half of a regular ax handle and its poll partly cleaned up with the aid of a grindstone. To collectors of these old discards from Kentucky's age of wood this is a familiar story. It arouses the kind of response displayed by more conventional antique collectors when they see a splendid spinning wheel daubed with white house paint and set out in a yard for display.

Thousands of "log" houses (actually built of hewn timbers) still stand all over the state, attesting to the skill of slick hewers who built them to last. The number of such structures is not readily apparent, for many of them are covered with aluminum siding or they are so well weatherboarded over that their true nature is effectively disguised. To see how much of a log in the round was hewn away to produce the building timber, one should look for a spot where the chinking between the logs has been removed. Here a rounded edge reveals the outer surface of the original log, sometimes with the bark still on, not uncommonly showing that a timber a foot and a half or more from edge to edge was hewn down to a relatively dainty five- or six-inch thickness.

With the decline of the building of homes from the majestic stands of yellow poplar and other beautiful Kentucky woods—brought on by impoverishment of forests and increasing popularity of frame construction—a newer and less glamorous use of the broadax developed. The nation's railroads needed millions of crossties, useful forest products that could be hand-hewn from second-growth timber. All over the state, during periods when labor was cheap, sturdy Kentucky woodsmen hewed railroad crossties by hand, keeping the old-fashioned broad-

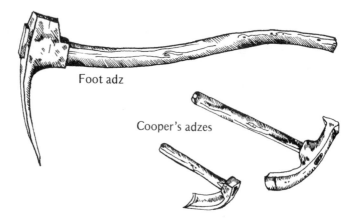

Foot adz

Cooper's adzes

ax at work in hundreds of localities across the state as recently as the great depression of the 1930s.

Mortised joists and rafters in old houses show some precise fitting that could not be done with ax, broadax, or saw; here is the work of expert craftsmen wielding adz and mortising chisel. Like the ax, the adz is an ancient tool, created in stone before the bronze age and widely known wherever man has worked in wood. Essentially, it is an adaptation of the ax, its cutting edge set at a right angle to the plane of the cutting edge of an ax. Whereas the ax generally serves to chop across the grain, the adz more frequently gouges out chips with the grain, having some of the same chisel characteristics of the broadax and performing the same dressing function with a lighter touch.

Because this dressing function is important in a variety of crafts, the adz appears in many forms. The cooper alone had a number of adzes especially designed to perform the specialized hewing of his trade. The standardized carpenter's adz is shaped to permit the workman to stand on the timber and use his own weight to control splitting. This dictates working with a heavy, razor-sharp cutting edge quite close to his feet. If his control is not good, or if his tool slips around a dense knot, he can easily hurt himself. There are anecdotes about adzmen tying barrel staves to their shins like a baseball catcher's shinguards to prevent injury when they are doing rough work. The assist the worker gets from his feet accounts for the traditional designation of *foot adz*.

Another observation of the loss of traditional skills and even associated verbal lore among people today comes from a recent auction. Among the tools being auctioned off were the two cooper's adzes illustrated. The smaller adz has a handle only about six inches long. It has a curved cutting edge suitable for dressing out convex surfaces, and it is a good example of old-fashioned blacksmith work in that the hardened steel cutting edge is "halfsoled" to the softer body. The auction was attended principally by farmers and other neighbors in a rural area. When the auctioneer came to the adzes, someone in the crowd asked, "What are they?" The auctioneer was at a loss. Finally an older bystander showed his superior knowledge by naming them. "Foot adzes," he exclaimed. His incorrect designation revealed that the one kind of adz he recalled was the common carpenter's adz, and, not understanding the function of the operator's feet in the use of that tool, he apparently assumed that the word *adz* is always associated with *foot*.

When the froe and froe club (or mallet) came up for sale, everyone appeared to be familiar with them. Kentuckians use enough tobacco sticks to keep the use of froe and club alive, but even this simple woodworking task is on the wane. An article in the August, 1975, *Kentucky Agricultural News* displays a picture of a Jackson County farmer riving tobacco sticks. The accompanying text explains that most people are now using machine-sawn sticks in spite of their recognition that the hand-split variety is superior.

Examination of a few dozen froes will show considerable variety in width, length of blade, size of eye, and kind of handle. This variety arises from the simplicity of the tool and its wide usage; great numbers of froes were

13

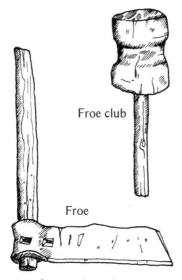

Froe club

Froe

handmade by ordinary people who possessed ordinary skills. Any convenient strap of iron of sufficient weight and size will do. It need only have one end turned over to form an eye that will accommodate a short hand-whittled handle. Temper is not critical because the froe should not be sharp enough to cut into the grain of the wood. Its function is to split along the grain, like a wedge. Once started with the blow of a wooden club the froe will follow the grain, opening the crack as the operator twists the blade sideways by levering it along with the handle.

The tool and its operation seem so simple that the novice is tempted to try. He discovers that something is lacking: the specialized knowledge communicated by an experienced workman. This is the knowledge once so common that it was reflected in everyday speech. "Dull as a froe" had meaning for people who used the tool and knew it should be dull. The proverbial simile is dropping out of everyday use, just as the tool is.

How deceptively simple use of the froe seems was clearly illustrated when a university film crew tried to make a documentary film showing old-fashioned tools and their use. A husky young farmer volunteered to demonstrate the froe by splitting a few white oak roof-boards. Two older men who attended the preview of the film broke into chuckles when they saw their young acquaintance wrestling with the froe and a tough white oak billet that refused to split cleanly into suitable shakes. "Reckon we ought to show that boy how to split a board?"

one of them asked the other. They then gave a brief catalogue of the performer's errors.

First of all, not just any tree trunk will split easily. The experienced woodsman sets aside for firewood the kind of shake bolt the film crew used. With expert eye he notes a straight, well formed tree without limbs close to the ground or other distortions. When he finds such a tree he sets the good portion of the trunk aside so that he can quarter it and split out the heartwood and sapwood, leaving clean, straight-grained bolts of uniform quality. He transports his raw material to an appropriate working site where he has set up a "brake," which is a large fork of a tree having limbs like the V of a slingshot spreading very gradually from the crotch. His brake is heavy enough to stay in place under the stress of ordinary leverage, and it is staked so that one limb is above the other at an angle that permits the billet to stand on the ground between the limbs and be supported against leverage from the side. Because the limbs angle from the crotch outward, the workman can choose the spot most appropriate for the thickness of the piece he intends to split.

If he does not have a proper club, he can make a suitable one in a few minutes. He chooses a section of a small, tough tree, preferably dogwood because of its fibrous, non-splitting quality. He whittles down one end to a size suitable for a handle and leaves a few inches of the other end in the round. Even a dull froe, simple as it seems, is a metal tool, not to be struck by another metal tool. With his materials and tools thus assembled, the boardmaker goes to work.

Cedar prop

Forked oak

Brake

He starts the froe with his

dogwood club. Once the split begins, he turns the froe to spread the crack and works it down into the billet. The split begins to run out at the side. The worker expertly reverses the pressure exerted by the brake against the side and guides the split back into the desired direction. In a sense, his brake is performing the same function as the feet of the adzman. The old-time hewer and carver knew how to control and use splitting, whereas most moderns are likely to be helplessly frustrated when an uncontrolled split follows the grain in a direction not intended. An experienced boardmaker recalled the work with relish: "Oh, I just loved to split boards. If I got the right kind of stuff, those boards just *plinked* off, pretty as you please. I could just stand all day and plink 'em off."

What has been called here a froe club is really one of many kinds of mallets. Because this mallet is club-shaped, it is more commonly called a club than a mallet. The traditional worker in wood uses so many hand tools in so many kinds of operations that he devises slightly different striking tools for special purposes. The carpenter's mallet illustrated is ordinarily made of beech or maple. It is suitable for striking other wooden tools without damaging them.

Mallet

Besides weatherboards, shakes, and tobacco sticks (which have dozens of uses besides their primary function), other useful objects can be split out of straight timber with a froe. Fragments of old slat-and-wire fences are a reminder of a skill not fully appreciated by a generation that buys fencing, sometimes even fence posts, at the hardware store. The old-fashioned rail fence was, of course, entirely a forest product, and its prodigious consumption of timber was not extravagant as long as timber was surplus and hardware was in short supply. The slat-and-wire fence gets most of its bulk from local timber, but it makes more efficient use of the forest and combines

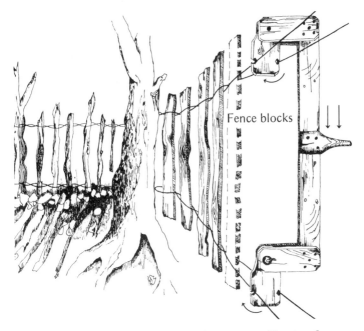

Fence blocks

smooth wire with the slats to make a very effective fence. It requires teamwork of two or more men. They carry ax, saw, froe, froe club, and rolls of smooth wire to the job. They cut suitable trees as they go along and split out the slats as they are needed. In this way they exploit local timber and do some clearing of the fencerow. Two wires at the top and two at the bottom criss-cross to weave the slats into place.

At another Kentucky auction the obviously homemade wooden contraption illustrated here came up for sale. It puzzled the auctioneer and most of the customers. One elderly bidder bought the tool because he recognized its function, remarking nostalgically, "Many is the day I turned the blocks to weave the wire on a slat-and-wire fence." The tool is a set of fence blocks. The short sections at each end are bolted on loosely so that they can rotate freely. They are spaced so that the distance between them is the distance between the top and bottom wires of a fence. Each of the rotating end sections has a small inlet cut into each side to accommodate a fence wire, so that the blocks can keep four wires in position at once. If the operator lifts the whole tool, the end sections flip down, causing the wires to cross. If he lowers the tool, the end sections flip up, causing the wires to cross in the opposite direction. Thus one man can perform with one hand a weaving operation that would require at least four hands unaided by the tool.

The fence blocks remind us that in the great age of traditional woodcrafts a workman could and did make many of his own tools. If necessary, he could invent and fabricate a tool for a particular problem. Ordinarily he made his simple tools within a tradition of design that had developed out of trial and error. But even though his general design was not original, his execution was, so that no two products are ever quite the same. They will vary according to the skill and aesthetic appreciation of their maker. Even the same craftsman will vary in his fabrication of a particular kind of object, depending on his mood, the quality of material at hand, the time he has to spend, whether he is making it for himself or someone else, and a host of other influences. Even a simple milk stool may be an aesthetic expression or a botched job!

The froe is simply a splitting tool to produce undressed pieces of wood of various dimensions. Its strong association with roof shakes probably derives from the large number of pieces on a roof and the large number of roofs to cover. The split shake roof is strongly defended over the roof covered with uniformly sawn shingles. If wood is split along its natural grain the rough surface is composed of many small ridges and grooves, which act as natural miniature gutters to convey rainwater. The shingle sawed across the grain lacks these natural grooves and tends to soak up rainwater.

Shakes, or roofboards as they are often called in Kentucky, are often in need of minor dressing to remove irregularities that would prevent tight application. The necessary dressing is accomplished with a drawknife, and the workman traditionally uses a shaving horse, still another example of a handmade object that any good workman can put together out of forest products at hand. Though the shaving horse has endless variation, its basic function is always

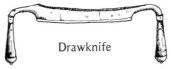

Drawknife

the same. It permits the worker to sit comfortably facing his work, and it holds the work with a simple vise arrangement so that the worker has both hands free for his tools. The shaving horse is close kin to the chair vises or horses used by cobblers, broom-makers, harness-makers, and others. Though the cobbler's bench or harness-maker's vise may be neat and compact enough to refinish and display in a living room (or even to be imitated in modern pseudo-antique furnishings) the shaving horse is too bulky, too heavy, too rough to have that kind of appeal. Essentially, it is a heavy bench made of the split section of a log, flat side up, supported on wooden legs. The log has a rectangular hole about three by eight inches cut through its approximate center. Fixed vertically through the hole and held by a loose wooden pin is a timber extending almost to the ground below and far enough above the surface of the bench to hold a heavy block of wood

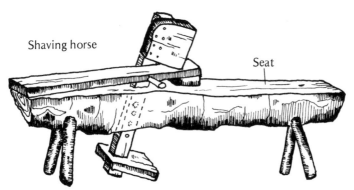

Shaving horse

Seat

fastened to its side. When the workman sits astraddle his shaving horse and pushes the movable upright piece with his foot, the block at the upper end of the timber swings down and clamps the work to the surface of the bench. When he releases his foot pressure the block rises and releases the work. There are many ingenious modifications and adaptations of this simple basic design.

A walk through an old-fashioned farmstead typical of hundreds of others reminds the viewer in many ways that wood skills and the time to use them were the principal factors in its development. The house illustrated here is about a century and a half old. It is made of hand-hewn yellow poplar timbers with half-dovetail corner notching. The logs for the timbers varied between twelve and

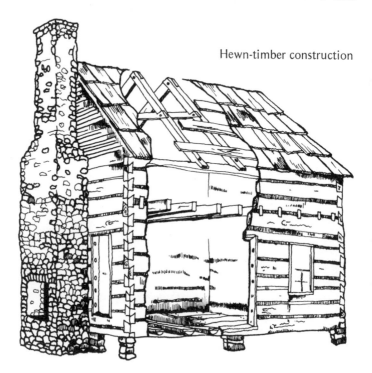

Hewn-timber construction

eighteen inches in diameter, and they were hewn down to a relatively uniform six-inch thickness. The building is a story and a half, making an upstairs with full headroom down its center under the roof peak and decreased head-

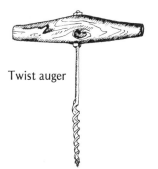

Twist auger

room at the sides, where the outside wall is only four logs above the joists. The joists, also of yellow poplar, are hand-dressed timbers exposed as beams in the ceiling of the downstairs room. They are mortised into the plate timbers. The upstairs floor is made of hand-dressed poplar boards laid over the joists. There is no ridgepole. The heavy rafters are lap-jointed at the peak and reinforced by mortised collar beams. Both the peak and collar beam junctures are fixed with wooden pegs.

A modern carpenter equipped with power drill and precision bits has no hesitation about boring holes in wood wherever they are needed. He would minimize this operation if his tool kit provided only the relatively slow and cumbersome hand-operated auger. Nevertheless, wood craftsmen have used augers in a remarkable range of activities. One reason that the auger has so many uses is that holes bored in wood are necessary for a variety of fastening or joining techniques involving pins and wedges. In the absence of hardware fasteners, workers in wood habitually thought of pinning or wedging to hold wooden pieces in place or to fasten them together.

Practically every detail of the old house represents hand crafting and hand fitting with ax, broadax, adz, auger, mortising chisel, and saw. The basic structure shows less deterioration after its many generations of occupancy than one finds in some modern frame constructions in their first decade. Truly, reconstituted woods, plywood, drywall, staple guns, pneumatic hammers, and power saws are vastly superior for mass production, but they do not necessarily produce sounder buildings.

Standing outside the old house one observes that it has a roof of rusty corrugated metal, a lean-to frame kitchen of some relatively recent construction, and a shed porch in need of repair. These are the do-no-better efforts of a recent generation. The makeshift appearance of these additions affects even the noble solidity of the original house. To appreciate the difference, one would have to strip off the roof and replace it with hand-riven roof-boards, or shakes, tear away the ugly frame rear addition, and rebuild the front porch. To get the sense of shifting values in handcrafts, however, one would do well to leave the house as it is. The original house accurately reflects the pride and skills of a generation of hewers and carvers who settled the land, a generation who built as though their houses should last forever; its present condition reflects the haste and frustration of the generations who used the old house without appreciation and tried to extend its function with tin, tarpaper, scrap lumber, and plywood. The exterior fireplace opening once faced into the room of a matching second half of the original structure. When that half deteriorated beyond usefulness it became firewood. Not surprisingly, this pattern is repeated in the history of many other old buildings. It is tempting to speculate that the people who blindly patched and exploited them, wringing out the last bit of use without putting anything substantial back in the way of upkeep, are also those who depleted the soil and allowed the hills to erode until there was nothing better to do than move out and get a factory job in the city.

Behind the old house is a small log structure once used as a smokehouse. It is clearly not as old as the house, yet its roof is falling in and the saddle-notched corners have slipped askew. Simple saddle notching of logs in the round for barns, smokehouses, and other outbuildings is accomplished with an ordinary chopping ax. The

22

builders obviously did not consider these structures as important or permanent as the dwelling house.

Still farther from the dwelling is a pole frame tobacco barn with a corrugated metal roof and unpainted vertical weatherboards. This is clearly a recent structure. Rust on the roof and warping boards suggest a limited life. Still, examination of its internal pole frame shows that some country craftsman hewed the poles into close-fitting timbers at critical junctures with a broadax. To that degree at least, handcrafting skills have persisted in the neighborhood. Those warping oak boards on the outside, rough-sawn in a neighborhood sawmill, will be the first to go. Only when the roof leaks or the weatherboards are far enough gone to let in moisture will the hewn framing timbers begin to sag.

Pegged door frame   Half-dovetail notching

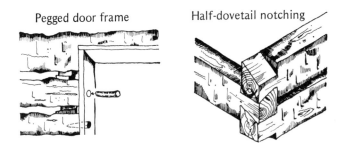

Most of the fencing in sight is ordinary barbed wire strung on home-cut cedar posts. Out behind the little family burial plot, however, there is an old section of slat-and-wire fence, yet another reminder of self-sufficient, time-consuming ways. The slat-and-wire fence cost more hours than money, was humane and hog tight. It required certain skills and the same methodical persistence that produced the hand-dressed poplar beams and puncheon floor in the dwelling house.

Since people in the neighborhood quite commonly use such locutions as "plumb worn out" and "honest and square," it is instructive to reflect on the values such figurative speech suggests. The values of a traditional worker in wood who built structures like this one stressed durability and solidity. These qualities can be seen in the buildings themselves. Prominent among the builder's tools were the plumb bob and framing square. Working without standardized lumber dimensions, without precut or prefitted parts, without blueprints and sophisticated measuring devices such as a transit, the timber hewer nevertheless made sure of perpendicular accuracy with his plumb bob and followed up with straightedge and framing square. His building may have lacked novelty and frills, but plumb and square it was. To use "plumb" as an adjective, then, came to mean "completely, perfectly, or altogether," and "square" came to mean "honest" or "right." Recollection of these tools conjures up images of workmen moving methodically on a deep carpet of curly shavings, chips, and sawdust, squinting with one eye along a straightedge or waiting patiently for the bob jiggling at the end of its string to settle. One contemporary owner of a solid, honestly built (plumb and square) house of that era remarked humorously of an exceptionally painstaking detail, "It must have taken one hundred hours, twenty tall tales, and ten pounds of chewing tobacco to get it done!"

3

EVERYDAY OBJECTS
IN WOOD

THE STORY of a miller's meal paddle illustrates the idea that neglected artifacts yield insights into the ordinary way of life of ordinary people. The old wooden object hanging on a nail in a neglected woodshed may tell part of the story of Kentucky just as effectively as a guided tour at a park or shrine. A curious customer at a Western Kentucky auction noticed a dusty, worm-eaten slab of wood hanging on a nail. The slab could have been a hand-riven white-oak roofboard, but two holes had been whittled near one end. The piece of wood (illustrated here) could be held firmly by inserting a thumb in the smaller hole, the fingers in the larger hole. But why? A child's attempt to make a painter's palette? A scraper of some kind? No one at the auction knew. Indeed, the piece would have remained undisturbed, hanging on its rusty nail as it had hung for many years, if the curious customer had not taken it down and asked that it be auctioned. He paid his fifty cents and carried away his puzzle. When he showed it to a friend old enough to recall carrying a turn of corn to the mill, the friend immediately exclaimed, "What are you going to do with that meal paddle?" Other old-timers gave the same kind of response: "Where did you get the paddle?" "What do you want that old thing for?"

In the gristmill, once at least as common a commercial establishment as a country crossroads store, the miller used a flat paddle to rake down grain as it came from the spout, to toss grain back into the hopper as he adjusted the stones, and to level the meal in his toll box. Almost any flat object would do, but the convention of the miller's paddle with thumb and finger holes whittled to the individual's desired size and design became so firmly established that the casually flourished object elicited immediate recognition and response.

Having established the identity of the meal paddle, its purchaser offered it to the Kentucky Museum at Western Kentucky University. The curator checked his inventory, found that the museum did not have one, and gratefully accepted the gift. The museum had a good stock of spinning wheels, Shaker chairs, ox yokes, and similar showy and conventionally collected artifacts, but no one had

Meal paddle

even thought of a meal paddle as an artifact that could call up memories of past institutions. The meal paddle, incidentally, reminds us of other homely wooden devices that were common at a time when the Kentuckian whipped out his pocketknife to produce a needed utensil. Think of butter paddles, apple butter stirring paddles, churn dashers, and sorghum skimmers to begin a long list of traditional designs.

When an urbanite moved into his newly purchased country home he decided to clear away the old cobwebby trash in the barn. He gathered up bits of harness, mouse-eaten horse collars, broken tobacco sticks and similar odds and ends to put in the fire he had built for their disposal. One common looking piece of wood puzzled him, however, for it had a harness snap fastened to each end. The piece was a little longer and a little heavier than a tobacco stick. He turned it over thoughtfully, uncomprehendingly. At that moment a neighbor walked in and remarked, "Hey, that's the first gee stick I've seen since I sold my mules!"

In the ensuing conversation the neophyte learned that a gee stick is used to train an unbroken mule or horse to harness. One end of the stick is snapped to the hame ring of a dependably trained animal; the other end is snapped to the bit of the trainee. When the obedient animal turns on command, the rigid stick "leads" the untrained one. The "gee" designation derives from the conventional "gee" and "haw" teamster terms. Even this seemingly uncomplicated bit of team lore turns out to be complicated by variation, such as bit-to-bit hookup for an untrained team or a bit-to-hame hookup for a single animal.

The neophyte changed his mind about throwing away the stick. Impressed by its name and function, he hung it up in the company of a ring maul, loom shuttle, and shoe last—all homely artifacts, all visible bits of Kentucky history. As with the miller's meal paddle, a bit of knowledge brought recognition, transforming a neglected piece of trash into a treasured souvenir.

Some schoolteachers have taken up this idea. They find that they can enrich their social studies classes, provide constructive activity and interest, and develop rapport with parents by letting their students bring in objects for other students to identify. Something like a gee stick or a meal paddle can start a guessing game, lead to elementary research, and provide topics for writing or discussion. One enterprising junior high teacher stimulated her students to set up a kind of fair in the classroom, complete with labels and explanatory texts for the display.

Kentucky folklorist Gordon Wilson remarked to some students in 1967 that he had not seen any basketmakers for several years. He wondered if this ancient craft, once a flourishing activity supplying roadside stands for the Mammoth Cave tourist traffic, had died out. Such a remark is sometimes taken as a challenge, and soon the students began reporting on active basketmakers, some of whom were weaving white-oak feed baskets in a fashion quite similar to the way their forefathers had.

The large bow basket made by weaving flexible strips or "splits" of white oak through rigid framing bows of the same material is still a common container on Kentucky farmsteads. Properly cared for, such a basket seems to last forever, acquiring a rich, dark brown patina with passing decades of use. Bow baskets range in size from a relatively dainty "egg" basket to a massive "bushel" basket. Some families prize an old basket as a family keepsake rather than as an antique: "It's the basket Granny always gathered eggs in."

A university film crew descended one day on Mrs. Francine Alvey, a frail-looking woman in her seventies living in the tiny community of Wax on the shores of

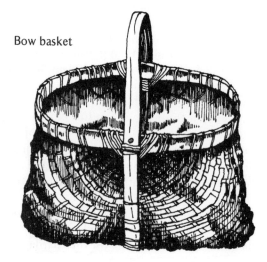

Bow basket

Nolin Reservoir. The film crew persuaded Mrs. Alvey to demonstrate the basket-making skill she had learned from her father, a skill she was still using to supplement her small social security income. Mrs. Alvey complied, and the result is a much prized short documentary film, which shows in great detail the production of one of our most traditional wooden artifacts, the bow basket. Mrs. Alvey has died since that production, but her contribution lives on as the film is viewed by thousands of Kentucky school children each year. Students who see the film

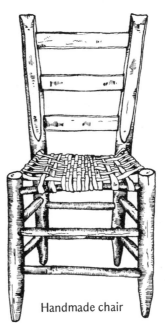

Handmade chair

learn how a froe works. In spite of her apparent frailty, Mrs. Alvey had no trouble splitting long white-oak saplings with that versatile tool.

Chairmakers, like basketmakers, were once found all over the state; like the basketmakers, they create a useful, durable product, using the raw materials directly from the forests shaped by simple hand tools. Like basketmakers, chairmakers have become enough of a rarity to be sought out by students and collectors. The chairmaker's tools are saw, ax, froe, auger, drawknife, and shaving horse. Ordinarily these are complemented by a simple lathe for turning posts and rounds. The lathe itself, if used, has often been another homemade tool, hand or foot powered. Employing traditional knowledge about the characteristics of compatible woods, the chairmaker produced a stout, durable chair without the aid of glue or nails.

In spite of obvious similarities in utility chairs such as

Hay rake

the simple ladder-back and woven bark or split seat
shown in the chair illustrated, close observation yields a
long inventory of minor differences. These include
straight and tapered leg ends; plain and ornamented back
posts; straight and curved back slats; straight and curved
back posts; posts in the round and posts flattened on one
side; and a variety of methods for weaving and fastening
the hickory bark or oak splits to form the seat. There are
differences also in the chairmaker's choice of materials.
One contemporary chairmaker who learned the craft from
his father uses only the wood of the sugar maple. Others
show preference for hickory, oak, and ash in a variety of
combinations. Fitting seasoned rounds into relatively
green legs is widely practiced to take advantage of the
natural tightening of the fit that comes with shrinkage.

An elderly widow's care of six of these chairs reveals
her appreciation of the simple, natural beauty of un-
masked wooden furniture:

We got them when we were married about sixty years ago. I
forget the name of the man who made them. I always took good
care of them, and they're as sound now as when we got them. My
niece got after me to get some paint and let her paint them but I
wouldn't do it. Every summer I would take them outside and
scrub them with sand and then set them out to bleach in the sun.
They always stayed so white and nice.

Some useful implements made of wood were relatively unmodified pieces except for holes bored to fasten them together. The principal modification of the wooden pieces of the hay rake was to bore a row of holes along one side of a block of wood for inserting the teeth, and a pair of holes at right angles to these for inserting the handle. The handle is a six-foot section of a hickory sapling split about a third of its length so that the two halves of the split portion can be inserted into the two holes bored to admit them. Wooden wedges hold the handle securely in place. The teeth are hand whittled to fit snugly into the row of holes bored to receive them. Wooden wedges secure the teeth. If a tooth breaks or wears out, the user simply whittles a new one and wedges it in place. The rake has no metal or manufactured parts, and its design is so simple that anyone with an auger, a pocketknife, and access to wood can make one. It illustrates perfectly the importance of both the auger and the wedge.

The calf yoke also derives its functional shape principally from the size and position of holes bored through a block of wood. The yoke is hung on a rogue calf's neck to keep it from climbing through fences. The example shown here is a short section of a sycamore limb with three holes bored through it. The paired holes hold a hickory bow made by cutting a green sapling and bending it into a U shape. The short piece of hickory fastened in the middle hole projects down far enough to bar the calf wearing the yoke

Calf yoke

31

from squeezing between fence wires. This effective device is made of three rather ordinary pieces of wood modified by an auger.

The naturally hollowed tree, often a sycamore, can serve as a temporary shelter, a well curb, a beehive (sometimes called *bee gum*), or a container. The bee gum illustrated is a section of naturally hollowed tree about two feet long and eighteen inches in diameter. The beekeeper augered holes in its sides to accommodate sticks whittled to about the size of a man's middle finger. These can be inserted so that they reach all the way through the hollowed section and provide horizontal support for the comb. This sample clearly shows remnants of honeycomb attached to the inner walls and crosspieces. All it needs to be placed back in service is flat boards for top and bottom closure. Although the Department of Agriculture has tried to eliminate these inefficient, old-fashioned hive bodies, some beekeepers seem to feel that bees prefer living in a hollow tree and persist in their use of a section of tree trunk for a brood chamber even if they bow to progress to the extent of using a modern super over it. This is a strange sight, symbolic of customary practices: persistence of the use of a traditional object even when it is oddly mismatched with contemporary technical advancement.

The word *gum* derives from the frequent use of black gum logs. This tree often produces useful hollow portions, as its heartwood is prone to decay. As elsewhere in regional speech, once the association was established, the word *gum* was uncritically detached and applied to products of other species serving the same functions. One of the most obvious associations has been with beehives, hence bee gum, even for a factory-made hive!

The much larger section of a hollow sycamore log illustrated with the bee gum has a board bottom and a wooden hoop performing the same function as a barrel hoop. Knotholes are neatly patched with pieces of tin to make the whole section grain-tight. This *garner* (about

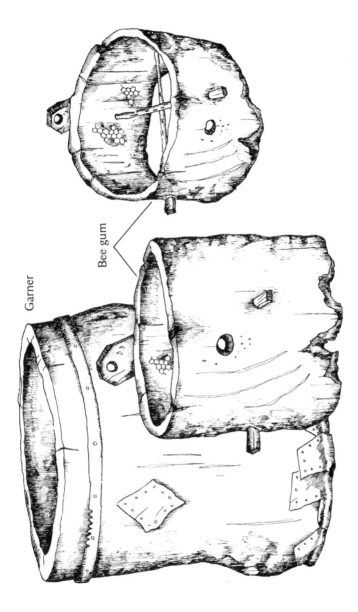

Bee gum

Garner

three feet in diameter) sits on the old threshing floor of the log crib at the center of a large, relatively modern barn. The owners recall that several such garners were once on the premises, but only one remains. The garners were once used for wheat storage. The persistence of the antique name for this antique storage is a point of interest. Such survivals of old-fashioned vocabulary are not uncommon. The term goes out of general use, but remains attached to the object (e.g., bee *gum*, fencing *blocks*, splitting *brake*, *poll* ax, *pump* log, *piggin*, *waling*). An interesting detail on the garner is a series of notches cut into the wooden hoop. They suggest a tally of some kind, but what? Bushels of wheat? Days worked? Years?

During the age of wooden ships, houses, vehicles, tools, and containers, the cooper's trade was much more important than it is in the age of glass, metals, and plastics. Modern Kentuckians are vaguely aware of the continuing use of charred oak barrels for aging bourbon whiskey. People not associated with the liquor industry would ordinarily be unaware of how the barrels are made or what they are worth. Yet there are living Kentuckians who recall earning spending money when they were boys by harvesting small saplings for the cooperage. The uniformly straight saplings were split and used for barrel hoops. One sees in a collection of old barrels the split sapling (with the bark on), the flat wooden split, and metal hoops, the choice depending on the period in which the barrel or keg was made and whether it was tight for liquid or slack for dry contents.

Good cooperage was beyond the skill of an ordinary handyman, for the complexities of angles and curves in a barrel call special tools and techniques into play. Even so, wooden pails, tubs, churns, and kegs were such familiar objects that anyone handy with tools might attempt to repair a broken stave or fit a new head, and some exceptionally clever whittlers could put together a reasonably good wooden vessel, such as the piggin illustrated. This container, a gift to the Kentucky Museum in

Bowling Green, originated in Edmonson County. It has one stave elongated to serve as a carrying or hanging handle. The wooden bands that form the hoops are fastened by means of a buttonhole arrangement, widely known and used in the era of wooden vessels. The bottom of the piggin, especially, shows the kind of hand whittling one would associate with nonjourneyman work, and two of the staves have flaws that would have been rejected by a professional cooper. The piggin is now so dried out that it is difficult to judge its original effectiveness as a liquid container, but there is no reason to doubt that it was tight enough to use.

Words like *piggin, noggin,* and *firkin* have a strange nostalgic impact in modern speech or writing, yet all of them designate familiar wooden vessels in their time, and *noggin,* in its modern slang use designating the head,

Buttonhole hoop

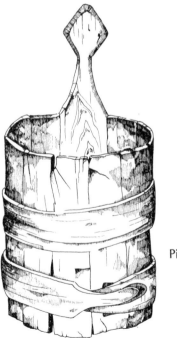

Piggin

recalls the nature of the vessel—a small wooden mug. Hence to get something into your noggin is to get something into your (wooden) head!

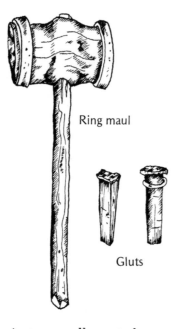

Ring maul

Gluts

Saving labor by using relatively unmodified natural forms extends to such obviously useful forest products as the tree fork and the naturally hollowed log. Minimal modification is seen in fence rails split from logs with maul and wooden gluts. Even the tools for rail splitting can be made from wood at hand and a little modification or addition. The glut is a wedge, easily cut out and shaped with an ax. The maul in its most elementary form is simply a heavy wooden club used to drive the wedges into a splitting log. Improvements on these tools consist of iron rings, a small one to keep a glut from splitting, a pair of larger ones for the familiar ring maul. At a time when much heavy work was done by hand, special variations of essentially the same tool evolved to fit the variety of its uses. Mauls, then, came in a wide range of sizes and shapes, partly to adapt to the job and partly to adapt to the stature and endurance of the user. One variety of maul is found in one piece, shaped like a froe club, but having a much heavier head and a handle about four feet long. A Warren County farmer of very small stature has a ring maul with a handle only half as long as the handle on a maul owned by one of his six-foot neighbors. One example has heavy hand-forged rings, which add weight to the head. Another has lightweight manufactured rings, apparently taken from a discarded wagon wheel hub. This richness of variety is a rough index of the usefulness of the maul in the age of wood.

Perhaps the crudest wooden tool on display in the Appalachian Museum at Berea is the flail. It is nothing more than a hickory sapling (about 82″ long and 1½″ in diameter) cut green, bent to nearly a right angle, and hardened in that shape. A flail is an ancient device for threshing out grain. Properly made, it permits the operator to stand in a comfortable position, gripping the flail at the end of the longer section, and strike the sheaves with a flat blade attached to the handle with a flexible hinge and swivel. The object is to distribute the blow along the whole surface of the blade, thereby knocking off the grain without shattering it. The Berea flail is crude, and it would not be very effective in its present dried-out state. But the supple fibers joining the two parts at the break were probably quite effective when the flail was green, performing some of the same functions as the leather hinge of more elaborately prepared implements. A well-made flail complete with swivel hood and leather thongs, incidentally, is not a common Kentucky artifact. The tool is ancient, but the historical development of agriculture in Kentucky came so close to the age of mechanical harvesting and threshing devices that the residue of hand tools for these activities is not as great as one might expect.

A flexible twig, shoot, or stem that can be twisted, tied, or woven is called a withe (pronounced *with*). Use of withes and

Flail

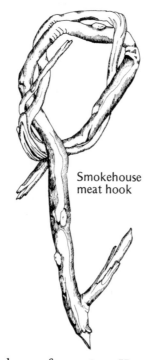

Smokehouse
meat hook

bark strings belongs largely to a frontier economy where wire and cordage are in short supply. It depends on an encyclopedic knowledge of the properties and practical applications of various trees and shrubs, the kind of knowledge that has become esoteric rather than common. The best known surviving application is seen in baskets and in hickory-bark chair bottoms.

A simple implement, but perfectly adequate for its purpose, is the meat hook illustrated. Cut as a green switch, it easily wrapped around the meat-hanging pole in a smokehouse and supported a ham or side of bacon for curing. Heat and smoke hardened it in this useful shape. Part of the Kentucky Museum collection at Western Kentucky University today, it still conveys the faint aroma of smoke-cured meat.

This minor piece of smokehouse equipment is a reminder that many people take the trouble to use wooden containers and wooden utensils for food storage and food preparation because of a set of popular beliefs relating to the "natural" quality of wood as contrasted with the "unnatural" quality of metal or other materials that do not occur ready to use in nature. This kind of preference persists to the present day, in which some people who have running water available at the kitchen sink still keep a wooden bucket of spring water and ladle it out with a gourd dipper. The use of cedar churns, wooden bread trays, wooden spoons, wooden apple butter stirring ladles, wooden equipment for butter-making, and a wide range of additional wooden kitchen and pantry ware—especially in an age of cheaper (and more sanitary) alternatives—reflects these values and beliefs. Ironically, what was once a necessity—a wooden utensil—has in some instances become a luxury in a later age in which wood is chosen for its aesthetic or romantic appeal.

Among the least modified pieces of wood selected for a useful purpose is the natural fork of a tree limb. The massive forked tree top trimmed and propped in place for a brake has its counterpart in the carefully selected Y of a branch for a boy's slingshot (*gravel-shooter* in Appalachia, *catapult* in England). The fork with a hole for insertion of a horizontal lever illustrated here is a *key* for tightening the ropes of an old-fashioned cord bed. This relatively unmodified fork appears to be just as useful and even stronger than the neatly whittled, symmetrical key also illustrated. A conjecture that the nails in the "face" of the more finished key are eyes in a fanciful mannikin toy

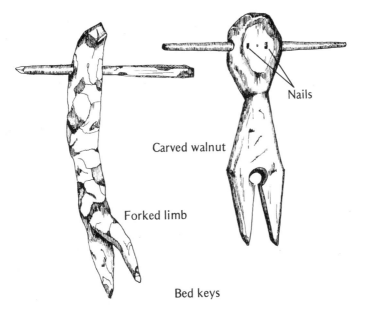

Nails

Carved walnut

Forked limb

Bed keys

would be correct. Other keys made to suggest arms, legs, and face have been observed.

The two versions of a common hand tool used in tobacco cultivation show how much difference there can be, even in the fabrication of a simple object. Both of the

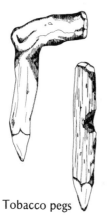

pegs shown have been used to set tobacco plants. The naturally curved handle and the harder, smoother wood of the peg on the left reflect care and skill. The rough, blunt, soft wood of the peg on the right suggests careless haste. It is a do-no-better peg. Very likely the inferior peg took its toll in extra effort and blisters. Very likely the small amount of extra effort ex-

Tobacco pegs

erted to make an attractive, effective peg paid off many times over in its conservation of energy in the field. A pointed stick is the most primitive agricultural implement. It is properly called a dibble, but few Kentucky tobacco farmers would use the word, now largely appropriated by anthropologists who use it to designate pointed sticks used in agricultural pursuits of a nontechnical society. In spite of its antiquity and simplicity, the dibble can hardly be improved upon for plant setting. Examination of a wide range of wooden artifacts like these supports the generalization that imaginative, skillful workers represent a minority, whatever the work may be. The disposition or maintenance of wooden artifacts suggests also that most modern people simply lack the knowledge to deal with them properly.

Once alerted to the utility of natural crooks and forks one begins to see them everywhere in old houses, barns, and sheds. The hanging bracket (also called *ceiling hook*) and wall hooks are in the Appalachian Museum at Berea.

In the barn large forks have been used as harness racks. In the house small crooks fastened to the wall become coat hangers. Larger forks are gun racks. To let nature do the work is a way to save labor, but there is an even more practical reason for using natural forms. Hooks or brackets sawn out of a plank are neatly uniform and symmetrical, but they are not strong. An irregular shape cut out of a seasoned timber can split along its grain when subjected to stress. It is for this reason that workers in wood sometimes seek out the portion of a tree that does not have straight, smooth grain. They want the tough cohesiveness of the root ball, burl, or forked branch for the durability its irregular grain provides.

Should one call a standing rack for hanging clothes a clothes tree or a hall tree? Reflection on these names may bring to mind other *tree* compounds such as doubletree,

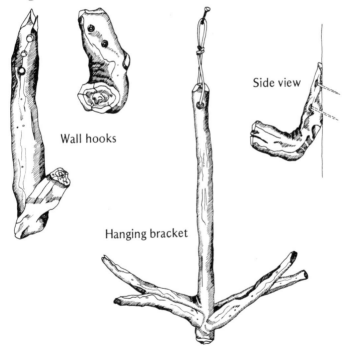

Wall hooks

Hanging bracket

Side view

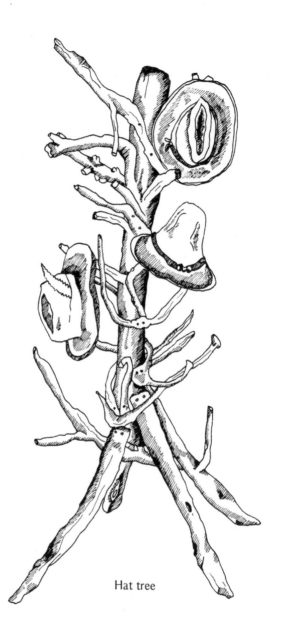

Hat tree

singletree, crosstree, and shoe tree. These may suggest still other vocabulary evidence of the importance of trees. Treenware, for instance, retains an older word for designating dishes or utensils made from trees. A large wooden peg used for fastening timbers is a tree nail (which became *trunnel* in its English language evolution). In any case, a natural tree is a natural choice for a place to hang clothing if one is outside. Indoors, an artificial tree must suffice. The standing hat tree shown here is an artifact of the age of wood housed in the Appalachian Museum at Berea. It is composed entirely of the kinds of naturally forked branches anyone can find in the forest.

4

EVERYMAN A MECHANIC

ONE GREAT ADVANTAGE of horse-drawn vehicles over automobiles is that any man reasonably handy with simple tools can maintain a wagon, whereas the average automobile driver is helplessly dependent on a specialist who, in turn, is helplessly dependent on factory-made replacement parts. When the deacon in Oliver Wendell Holmes's poem carefully selected lancewood, white-wood, ash, and logs from the "Settler's ellum," for his nearly indestructible one-hoss shay he was using the properties of various kinds of trees for their specialized functions. Many a Kentucky farmer would have chosen as well as the deacon, and he would have had as wide a range of raw materials to choose from. Though the rural blacksmith at many Kentucky crossroads doubled as a wheelwright, ordinary farmers maintained their own forge and anvil. They were perfectly capable of re-tiring a wagon wheel, replacing a wooden spoke, or even of fabricating a new felly. During off seasons and after hours for field work the provident, self-sufficient man put his time to good use by stockpiling ax handles, wheel spokes, shoe pegs, and singletree blanks so that they would be available when the need arose.

A new owner of an old barn came across a supply of stout, neatly carved, unused singletrees. All they lacked was the hardware, which can be removed from an old wooden stock and fastened to a new one. Puzzled by the unfamiliar wood, he asked a neighbor to identify it. "Bodock," was the answer, "real good wood for singletrees. Springy and strong." The unfamiliar term sent the inquirer to a dictionary, where he discovered that *bodock* designates Osage orange, commonly known as hedge apple, and is derived from the French *bois d' arc*. Familiar with archery, he recognized at once that any wood good enough to be preferred for longbows should be good enough for a singletree.

Just as Osage orange provides wood suitably springy for archery bows, other properly prepared wood finds application where elastic qualities are needed. The longbow achieved its highly specialized shape over centuries of use, and its efficient, powerful spring would inevitably suggest analogies. A spring consisting of an evenly tapered piece of seasoned wood has been applied to a variety of needs such as door and gate latches and ratchet-and-pawl mechanisms. A spring pole, clearly reminiscent of the archer's bow, provides reciprocal tension for the boom-and-treadle lathe frequently used by chairmakers and for opening the jaw of the kind of shaving horse that employs no counterweight for that purpose. Some contemporary shaving horses, incidentally, show adaptation to byproducts of modern technology in the substitution of innertube rubber bands for the spring pole.

Every year thousands of tourists at Mammoth Cave walk past remnants of the nitrate works down in the cave. A mimeographed handout prepared for cave visitors explains the ruins briefly:

NITRATE MINING OPERATION. In 1812 England blockaded our shores and invaded our lands. To keep the independence won just 30 years before, a war must be fought, and gunpowder was needed. All powder had been imported from Europe, and a local source had to be found. Miners went into caves to get the needed ingredient—nitrates. They constructed these vats, filled them with the cave earth that was rich in nitrates, and leached out the nitrates with water. Water came to the vats, and the brine solution was carried back to the entrance in wooden pipes bored by hand. These are all original timbers. Other caves helped produce nitrates during the war of 1812, but Mammoth Cave outproduced all others.

In addition to being an interesting historical site in Kentucky, these ruins, partially illustrated here, provide a remarkable display of early dependence on wood technology. Wooden pipes made by boring out oak and poplar logs conveyed spring water from the surface down into the cave. There the water percolated through the nitrate-rich cave soil and dripped from the leaching vat into a collecting trough below it. The nitrate solution was then raised through wooden pipes by a wooden pump so that the solution could be boiled down to produce the end product out in the open air. Only remnants of this extensive, complicated system remain in the cave, but even these are impressive evidence of what could be done with simple tools and good logs.

These ruins show a range of woodworking techniques. The drip trough under the leaching vat is a hollowed out section of the split half of a log. Such a container, made with ax and adz, may range from cattle watering troughs to bread trays and bowls. The same construction on a larger scale could produce a dugout canoe.

Between the drip trough and the vat above is a sloped layer of concave wooden strips laid like Spanish tile to hold the solids up and permit the solution to drip through. Above these is the large vat made of planks, sturdily braced with mortised cross braces to give it strength.

The pump logs (so called because they were used for wooden pump housings as well as for pipes) had their centers bored out by long hand-operated augers equipped with extensions for the bits. Anyone who has tried to bore into the grain instead of across it with a modern twist bit knows how difficult it is. People who made pump logs knew also, but they solved the problem

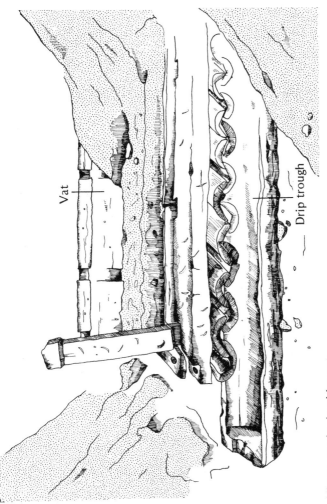

Vat

Drip trough

Nitrate works, leaching vat

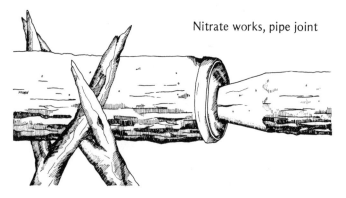

Nitrate works, pipe joint

by using several varieties of pod bits, especially designed to bore with instead of across the grain. The illustrated sections of log pipe were joined by tapering one end on the outside and reaming the other end on the inside. The sections were then driven together. An iron band on the reamed end of a section kept it from splitting. If by some irregularity the bit worked out the side of a log being bored, all was not lost. The workman simply cut off and used the short section successfully completed.

One is tempted to conclude that emergency need for

Nitrate works, pumping system ruins

gunpowder in the War of 1812 stimulated the invention needed for this ambitious piece of wood engineering. Actually, it illustrates the fact that pioneers in Kentucky brought a high degree of woodworking skill to a magnificently forested frontier where they could put their skill to work. Wooden pipes, even municipal wooden waterworks, were already established in Eastern cities before Kentucky settlement.

Wooden clockworks, also, were factory-produced in New England, but no manufactured clock is likely to excite wonder quite as much as the one illustrated here. It stands, quiet now, on display in the lobby of Park Mammoth resort, near Park City. It is a large, ungainly looking clock with some of its bulky wooden works showing through the cut-out center of its face. This typewritten description is mounted inside the glass door:

This clock was made about the year of 1800 by Van Dockery at the age of fourteen years. Van's parents emigrated from Virginia at the close of the Revolutionary War, and settled in what is now north Butler County, Kentucky. It was a wilderness at the time. Van was born there in a one-room log cabin. Schools being few and far between, he received very little education. He was fourteen years old before he ever saw a clock. One day a traveling preacher stopped at the Dockery home and he carried a watch. Van looked it over, and he conceived the idea of building this clock. He set to work with a kit of tools consisting of a one-bladed Barlow knife and a saw which he made from one of his mother's kitchen knives. He "whittled" the works of the clock from apple wood. The cabinet of the clock was also made by hand. A weight (22 pounds) was added. It took six months to complete the clock. Later, Van became a Jeweler and a Druggist.

This sketch was written by the Reverend B. F. Burden, a nephew, Beaver Dam, Kentucky.

A close look at the applewood cogwheels reveals that the clock worked for many years. The teeth are so deeply worn that they are noticeably asymmetrical. A still closer look reveals a remarkable repair. Three of the teeth,

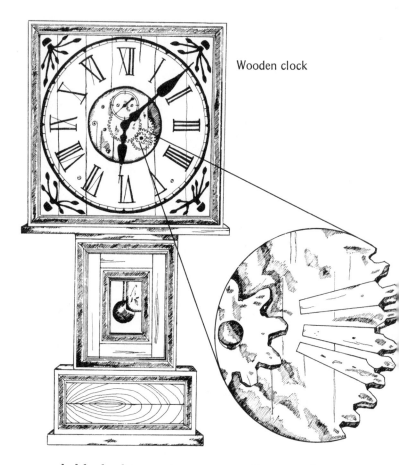

Wooden clock

probably broken or too worn to function, have been neatly excised and replaced. Such an operation required a clever, careful workman.

Because repair ordinarily requires less time than replacement, ingenious ways of fixing a broken wooden object attract attention. Skilled workers in wood could perform such a repair as the replacement of teeth in a clockwork, but those who came after them sometimes employed ridiculously ineffective makeshifts or gave up entirely.

A prize example of makeshift repair is seen in the much abused homemade cotton gin illustrated here. When it was offered at an auction in 1973, hardly anyone present knew what it was, and since it appeared ready to fall apart, it sold for less than two dollars. Its purchaser removed three mismatched screws, eighteen mismatched and mostly bent nails, one piece of wire, a rag, and a two-foot piece of fishline to get down to the basic structure so that he could begin to glue the broken parts together and repair the splits caused by the nails and screws. The cotton gin had been used (by people who had borrowed it!) with such vigor that they had broken some of its simple parts. To continue using it they had resorted to the repairs mentioned above, presumably until it was past further patching.

This kind of gin appears to be a homemade implement well known in some communities, unknown in others nearby. It is unlike the efficient Whitney invention in that it squeezes seeds out of the previously warmed fibers just as a clothes wringer squeezes water out of fabric. The secret of its operation is the small size of the rollers— about the diameter of an average adult's index finger. If the rollers were larger they would crush the seeds and carry them through with the fibers. The oak rollers are hand whittled and attached to hand-whittled poplar cranks. The bearing assembly has a primitive appearance, but it is ingenious and effective, maintaining firm alignment and adjustable pressure on the rollers. This is accomplished by whittling a groove in each roller to receive the edge of a poplar chip inserted through a slot cut into each of the side mounting brackets. The poplar chip, being softer than the oak roller, shapes itself to the groove when pressure is applied while the roller turns. The slot is long enough to allow insertion of a wedge-shaped poplar chip above each bearing. The tightness of the wedge dictates the firmness with which the roller surfaces are held together. This is the working assembly, one which may be mounted in several different ways.

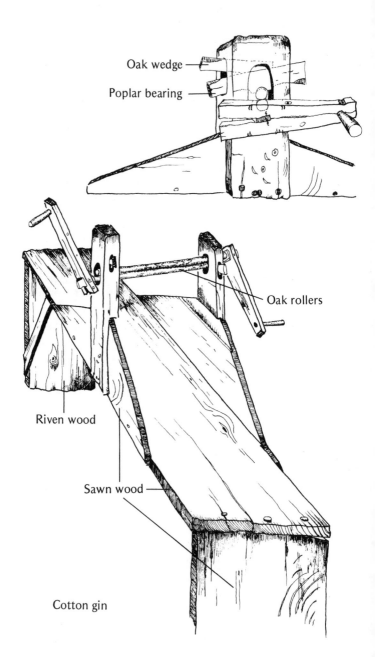

Oak wedge

Poplar bearing

Oak rollers

Riven wood

Sawn wood

Cotton gin

One of the gins shown has the assembly permanently mounted on a bench made of rough boards. An old photograph shows such a gin in operation, powered by two small boys, one sitting on each end of the bench, turning a crank. A third person is feeding the warmed cotton fibers into the gin.

This clever product of an unknown carver takes up some storage space. Another gin works on exactly the same principle, but has two improvements. It is a takedown model, convenient for flat storage. The working head is mortised through the center of a board about the same length and width as the bench of the first model. It extends through the board so that it can be fastened with a tapered wooden pin. When assembled, it can be laid across two chairs or any similar support for use. The other improvement is a piece of tin fastened below the rollers so that its edge will barely scrape the lower side of the bottom roller. This will scrape away the seeds as they are ginned out. It has the same adjustable yellow poplar bearings seen in the first model, but its white oak rollers

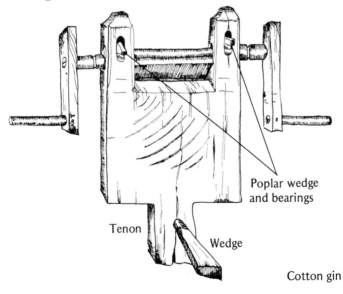

Poplar wedge
and bearings

Tenon

Wedge

Cotton gin

appear to have been turned on a lathe instead of whittled.

These two gins were used within five miles of each other. A third gin in the same neighborhood, not illustrated because its owner cleaned out her woodshed and burned it, had no seating arrangement. Instead, it was built on four legs spaced about the same way and the same height as the legs on a child's high chair. This placed the cranks at a convenient height for the operator to stand while turning them. An additional refinement was a box hung under the rollers to catch the seed. Reports of still other cotton gins in the same rural area indicate additional variations in detail.

Traditional expressions such as these are natural hold-outs against copyrights, assembly lines, and blueprints. There is no official or standard version of a ballad, fiddle tune, ghost tale, smokehouse, shaving horse, or gate latch. Because there is no original copyrighted version or set of plans, the individual always expresses his own version, even if he is following a model. If one hundred singers render one hundred different versions of a ballad, the differences would have to be in certain details, which can vary without destroying a necessary core of similarity by which we identify the song. Similarly, if one hundred whittlers make cotton gins, each one will differ from all others in some respects, yet all will have that core of similarity by which we identify the object. To be functional at all, the homemade gin must have rollers of particular dimensions and an appropriate framework to hold them for cranking. Beyond this functional specification the craftsman is free to embellish and improvise.

The clock discussed above shows careful repair by a skilled woodworker. The first cotton gin had been operated by unskilled people who resorted to nails, wire, and string to hold it together. When latter-day tenants of a fine old saddlebag house made of hewn poplar logs found that one half of the house was leaking badly and starting to rot down, they moved all their belongings into the sound side and cut up the logs of the defective side for firewood. Repair, or lack of it, provides some clues about declining skill and incentive. Three repairs tell three different stories.

The split part of a flaxwheel shows ingenuity and a kind of appropriateness in the choice of ferrule to hold the split sections together. A sewing thimble has been forced over the whittled-down shaft by some unknown repairman. The original wheel was attractively made. The repairman's coarse knife marks suggest haste, a desire to get the wheel working—and never mind its looks!

The old wooden bit brace would be prized by a collector if it were in better repair. The cutaway illustration shows the clever way the rotating button is held in place by a wooden pin fitting into a groove in its shank. A crack at this naturally weak point has been reinforced by fas-

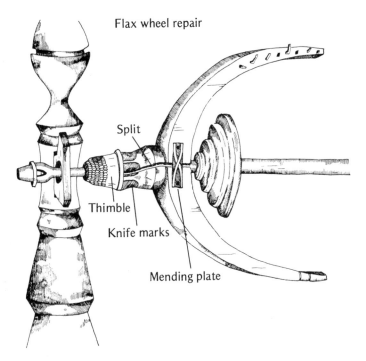

Flax wheel repair

Split

Thimble

Knife marks

Mending plate

tening a metal plate over the weakened area. Though this is apparently effective, it destroys the symmetry and finish of a tool originally designed to satisfy some aesthetic sensibility.

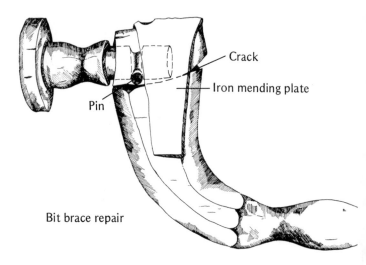

Crack

Iron mending plate

Pin

Bit brace repair

The hand-cut ratchet and pawl on the quilting frame is a simple mechanical device using a wood-to-wood fastener. The object is to keep a section of the quilt stretched tight between the two long rails that reach from one trestle to the other. The unquilted portion is rolled up on the locked rail at the right. As the quilters finish a "reach" they roll it up on the rail at the left, adjusting the tension and holding it by means of the wooden ratchet wheel. The walnut ratchet fits over the rounded end of the rail. It is locked in place by a wooden key, or spline, consisting of a small dowel fitting into a hole located so that the contact of the key is divided between ratchet wheel and the rail to which it is attached. The pawl has a loose fastening so that it will fall into locked position by its own weight. A wooden pin keeps it from falling beyond its operating position when the rail is pulled back or re-moved. The walnut trestles have no metal fasteners. All joints are mortised and pegged. The only metal is a row of carpet tacks holding a strip of outing flannel used to fasten the quilt in place on the first reach.

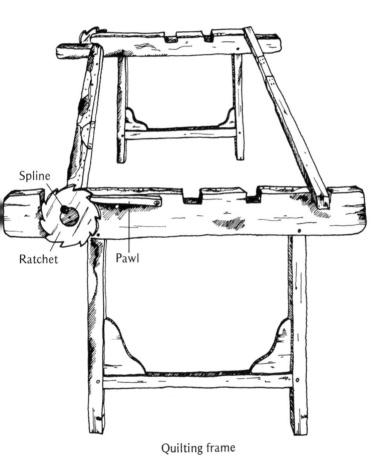

Quilting frame

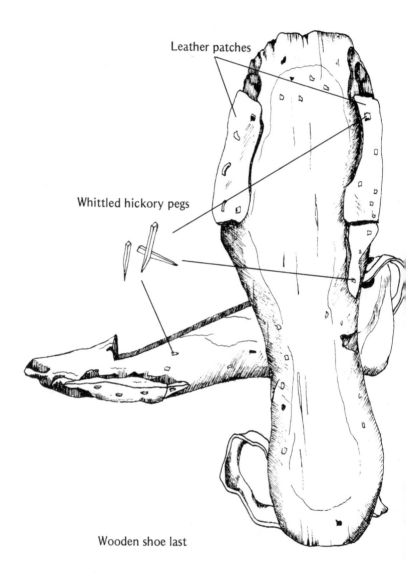

Leather patches

Whittled hickory pegs

Wooden shoe last

The mended wooden shoe last is a reminder that necessary frugality lay behind much of the woodcraft of an earlier era. Hardwood shoe lasts are usually factory made. Shoe repair was an ordinary household skill. The hand-whittled shoe peg is the smallest homemade wooden artifact. If Granddad had gotten too feeble to do anything else, he could sit by the fire and whittle shoe pegs. Sometimes a whole can or jar of these homely reminders of self-sufficiency will turn up on a dusty old shelf. Pegging down the uppers puts wear on the wooden last. Over the years its edge becomes more and more splintered and ragged, so that finally it loses its function as well as its substance. An unknown cobbler extended the life of the last illustrated here by mending it with scraps of leather. They are fastened with both metal shoe tacks and wooden pegs.

Ingenious uses of wedges, pegs, mortised joints, dovetail notching and other ways of joining or fastening is sometimes explained by the fact that hardware was once scarce enough to foster ingenious wood fastenings. This is only part of the explanation. An iron spike splits and tears the wood, then wears itself loose. Ultimately it rusts and creates a rotting cavity. A wooden peg in a mortised joint places compatible materials together—wood to wood—without trauma to the members being joined. The peg will not wear away the augered hole it is designed to fit, and it will not rust. The craftsman who uses pegs and wedges is familiar with their seasoning, shrinking, and splitting properties and makes allowances for them. Metal fasteners, like modern power tools, require less skill and time.

5

PLAYPRETTIES AND FUN

AFTER SATISFYING urgent needs such as housing for people and livestock, fencing pasture, providing implements and utensils for domestic activities, and logging for ready cash come less urgent needs such as amusement, pastimes for children, and aesthetic pleasures. In leaner times people depended on the same traditional skills and raw materials to satisfy these lesser needs.

Some observers of indigenous crafts have pointed out the careful attention given to personal adornment. The walking stick has more often been an adornment than an aid to walking. Gold-headed canes were affected by the well-to-do when canes were in vogue. The countryman often whittled his own or secured an unusual formation in the woods and improved upon it. A natural "decoration," for instance, is the spiral marking on a sapling parasitized by a climbing vine. Illustrated here are details from four canes in a collection at the Kentucky Museum in Bowling Green. One is decorated by a piece of deer antler; one has exploited a natural deformation for a handle, further improved by some whittling that gives it the shape of a boot heel; one has the ornate carved head fastened by a treenail pin. The boot heel cane has a 30-30 brass cartridge case for a ferrule. The prize of the lot is the copperhead cane formed by putting two unusual natural formations together with a well executed lap joint. This

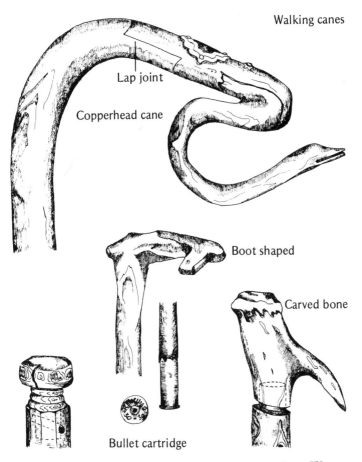

Walking canes

Lap joint

Copperhead cane

Boot shaped

Carved bone

Bullet cartridge

cane caught the fancy of Kentucky poet Jim Wayne Miller, whose first volume of published poetry bore the title *Copperhead Cane*, from the title poem. A serpent motif is fairly common on carved canes, probably because natural reminders are easily seen in the serpentine forms of some saplings and branches. These are selected and accentuated by the carver.

Very recent technology has deprived boys of an important source of raw material for toys: the rubber inner tube.

Modern synthetic tubes do not have a suitable snap for gravel-shooters and other toys that developed in the days of natural rubber inner tubes that could be had for the asking at any service station or garage. In the height of Kentucky's age of wood, however, the rubber inner tube had not yet made its appearance. Wooden tops were spun with strings or whips; pebbles were hurled with slings like the one David used against Goliath; and popguns shot pokeberries with disconcertingly messy accuracy.

The slingshot and sword illustrated here are in the Appalachian Museum in Berea. Whittling simple artifacts such as these has been a nearly universal experience of growing boys. Appropriately, the well chosen fork for the slingshot (gravel-shooter) is oak, whereas the wooden sword is poplar. Oak is stronger; the natural fork required little shaping. Poplar is easier to whittle, and the toy sword is not subject to shearing stress.

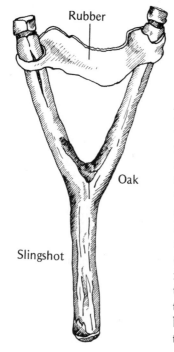

Rubber

Oak

Slingshot

The country popgun is a straight section of an alder branch about eight inches long with its soft center removed to form a tube. A suitable piece of wood is whittled to form a fairly tight-fitting—but freely plunging—piston which is long enough to travel most of the way through the tube and stopped by a handle of a larger diameter. The user inserts a ripe pokeberry (or other similarly pliable wad) into each end of the tube, then quickly rams the piston through the bore. The first berry makes a seal so that the air is compressed in the

Pencil lettering

TARJAN THE LINE KILLER

TARZAN

Toy sword

bore. The quickly compressed air, in turn, "pops" the second berry out of the far end with a report loud enough to satisfy the ears and velocity enough to sting (or splatter) a target several feet distant. The alder branch has a suitably soft pith for easy removal, and has, therefore, other functions, such as spiles for tapping sugar trees.

The fluttermill, a popular toy, combined the everuseful forked branch with the equally useful cornstalk. If the child had a small stream to power his mill, he set bearings on each side of the flowing water by pushing a small forked stick into the ground. He then cut a cornstalk shaft barely shorter than the distance between the bearings and extended it by inserting a wooden peg into the center of each end, allowing the pegs to extend far enough to rest on the forked sticks. He then cut slits all

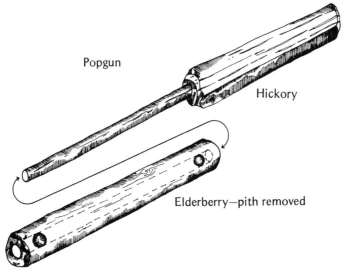

Popgun

Hickory

Elderberry—pith removed

the way around the center of the shaft and inserted cornstalk blades long enough to reach the running water. The result—a child's replica of an undershot mill wheel merrily splashing in the stream. Now that the real mill is only a memory for most people, the child's inspiration to make a fluttermill appears to be greatly diminished.

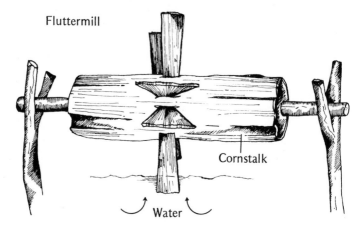

Fluttermill

Cornstalk

Water

Similarly, now that old-fashioned work involving props and wedges is no longer commonly observed by children, an effective humorous device for enticing a child away from a pout would not be readily understood. This is simply a forked stick, kept handy in the busy old-time household. Elders referred to it as a *lip prop.* Should a child pout enough to warrant response, an elder could offer to get the lip prop to aid the pouter; thus humor would serve better than a scold to restore harmony.

The wooden chain, the caged ball, or a combination of these will test the skill of a whittler. The combination illustrated here was whittled in 1927 by a Warren County handyman to amuse a young girl. His "puzzle" is intended to puzzle the observer. The parts are loose, but they cannot be disassembled. Authentic puzzles—that is, puzzles that can be assembled and disassembled, offering a challenge to both the user and the creator—are also in the whittling tradition.

Modern manifestations of these old whittling traditions can be seen in novelty weathervanes, mailbox stands, and animated figures such as limberjacks and pecking chickens, many of which reach back to early European analogues.

Observers at a 1973 Kentucky crafts festival could watch several skilled workers turn out wooden creations representative of their respective specialties. One who attracted much admiring attention was a young woman using an ordinary pocketknife to whittle wooden chains of remarkable length and uniformity. The pocketknife was the proper tool, and the chain is a favorite whittler's motif. The young woman might have drawn a crowd of admirers in any case, but it seemed clear that the novelty of a female whittler was at least partly responsible for the cluster of attentive observers.

A fairly common artifact of Kentucky's heritage which collectors have tended to neglect is the homemade grindstone. Good stones with appropriate grit and dimensions have long been available on the market, but even in recent years they have been an expensive luxury to some poverty-ridden country people. They satisfied their sharpening needs by locating a sandstone ledge having an adequately firm and uniform stone, quarrying out a disc, chiseling a square hole in its center, mounting it on a square wooden shaft, and mounting this assembly with a wooden crank handle. As recently as 1969 a Western Kentucky farmer complained that he had broken his well used homemade grindstone by hammering too hard while mounting his grindstone on a new wooden shaft.

The experienced worker in wood knows the value of a sharp tool. Methods and materials for sharpening ax, adz, drawknife, and pocketknife vary, but they have one thing in common: A high-speed mechanical grindstone is not suitable for any of them. How the old-timer winces when

Toys

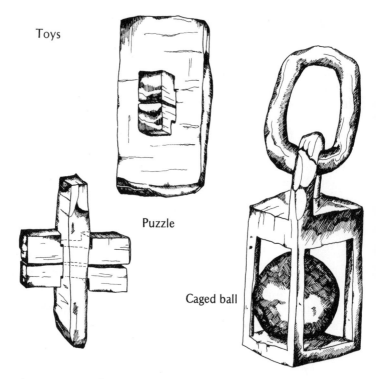

Puzzle

Caged ball

he sees an ax losing its temper in a shower of sparks at the grindstone! How he treasures the bit of "whetrock" he carries in his pocket to renew the perfect edge of his pocketknife! Both the use and the maintenance of old-fashioned hand tools are geared to an era not dominated by the time clock and construction schedule.

An anecdote about an employer's test of a prospective worker's worth preserves a common attitude about a man and his tools. While talking to the applicant the interviewer would invent an excuse to borrow the workman's pocketknife. If the applicant had a knife to lend, and if the knife proved to be a sharp, reliable tool, its owner was a good prospect. If he carried no knife, or if his knife showed neglect, he would not pass.

In Kentucky, whittling has been customarily reserved

for men and boys. Among the men it has been ordinarily accompanied by tobacco chewing and discussion of politics. Men still go to town on Court Day carrying a seasoned piece of poplar or cedar so that they will have something to whittle on as they participate in the elaborate, leisurely ritual of knife swapping.

6

LOGGERS, RAFTERS, AND SAWYERS

KENTUCKY HISTORIAN Tom Clark describes in *The Kentucky* the harvest of the forests, especially those in the drainage area of the Kentucky River. By the end of the Civil War, he writes, "Down in the Bluegrass lumbermen and cabinetmakers had systematically cut back the huge black walnuts, wild cherry, river bottom tulip, maple, buckeye, linden, and sycamore." Even so, logs further up the branches remained to be cut. Clark goes on to tell that a spring tide in 1871 destroyed 3,000 poplar logs cut along the Laurel Fork of Goose Creek, and as late as 1915, a tide carried away thousands of logs along the South Fork of the Kentucky. These dates and quantities of timber apply equally to other rivers—Big Sandy, Cumberland, Green—and even to creeks too small to float logs except during a "tide" of floodwaters.

Rafts for lumber, also loaded with produce, were floating down the Ohio destined for New Orleans toward the end of the eighteenth century, and large-scale rafting continued well into this century. Loggers and rafters had special skills and tools—even anecdotes and practical jokes. The modern reader whose closest acquaintance with a raft on the river comes from reading *Huckleberry Finn* may be tempted to romanticize the lean-to shelter and campfire in a sandbox. He may think of broad vistas, lazy days, swimming, fishing, and relaxation as the gentle river current carries the raft effortlessly to its destination. Actual accounts still readily available from experienced rafters tell a different story.

Felling and trimming trees by hand required stamina. Skidding logs to the creek or riverbank with horses or oxen was slow, frustrating work. When the logs went into the water to be strapped into tiers an occasional dunking (or even drowning) was inevitable. Loggers are necessarily a hardy lot, however, and in spite of danger and discomfort, found time for horseplay and tale-telling.

There is a numskull story about Uncle Billy, for instance. Uncle Billy was helping a crew roll logs into a branch to float them down to Barren River during freezing weather. He grabbed a brittle branch to steady himself, slipped, and fell in. His clothing began to freeze, so he hurried home, changed to a dry outfit, and returned to work. One of his companions asked, "Uncle Billy, how in the world did you do that?"

"Well, it was this way," Uncle Billy said, "I was standing right here and I reached out and grabbed the branch like this. . . ." He demonstrated and fell in again.

Once tied to a numskull routine, Uncle Billy inevitably got himself into another tale. This time he was skidding logs out of the woods with a log sled and yoked oxen. He had one end of a log up on the sled and the team ready to hook on when he dropped his clevis pin. To keep the clevis lined up he stuck his finger in the hole while he groped for the pin with his other hand. About that time a noise in the woods startled his team. The surge of the oxen against the chain neatly amputated Uncle Billy's finger.

A large raft requires substantial strapping to hold it together. This is a split sapling laid across the logs flat side down and pinned to the logs. What if a sapling is too large to be managed by a froe and too long to split conveniently with wedge and maul? One family of loggers had an answer. They sharpened a plowshare and fastened it vertically in the V of a handy tree crotch. They then trimmed the tree they wanted to split, opened the butt with a wedge, pushed the beginning split into the crotch to engage the plowshare, and hitched an ox to pull it through. As the ox pulled the sapling through, one of the men held its top to guide the split.

In the meantime, other workers had split wooden pins out of a suitable billet with a froe and dressed them on a shaving horse. The final step was to lay the strapping across the floating logs and bore holes through the strapping and into the logs to accommodate the pins. Once more, the investigator finds that special kinds of knowledge were required to make the operation successful. It was important to drive the pins firmly into the logs so that they would hold. It was equally important to avoid splitting and weakening the strapping. The problem was solved by using two augers, one for a slightly larger hole in the strapping, a smaller one for the tighter fit in the log. Some rafters enhanced that tight fit by driving a square pin into a round hole.

Those chain dogs the boy found on a derelict log raft represented a more recent era. They came into use when metal products became available, simplifying the process by eliminating the wooden pins and augers. Two steel wedges were driven into the log, one on each side of the strapping, the short section of chain that joined the wedges holding the strapping in place. At the end of the trip the rafters could knock all the hardware out of the raft and carry it back upriver for the next trip. The all-wood fastening had one great advantage in that there was no metal to be overlooked. Even a single spike can play havoc with the machinery in a sawmill.

The saw is an ancient tool, but good saws were imported from European manufacturers until the early years of the nineteenth century. They were an expensive luxury at the time of first settlement, which accounts for

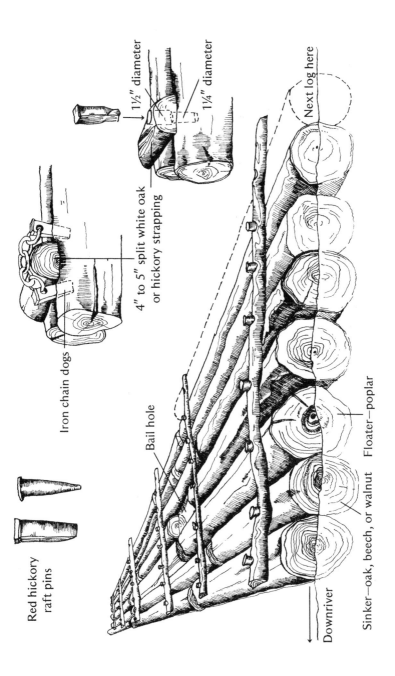

Red hickory raft pins

Iron chain dogs

4" to 5" split white oak or hickory strapping

1½" diameter

1¼" diameter

Bail hole

Next log here

Downriver

Sinker—oak, beech, or walnut

Floater—poplar

so much early dependence on the ax. Furthermore, one man can work with ax, wedges, and maul, whereas it takes two to pull a crosscut saw. Expert splitting can produce usable boards and framing timbers that would consume too much labor to saw out by hand, even in an era of cheap labor.

Between the split board and the board from a sawmill, many Kentucky communities experienced an interim phase. Needing some sawed-out planks and lacking a power mill, the pioneer resorted to an ancient, man-killing device, the pit saw. This is a long, coarse-toothed saw somewhat like a crosscut saw but distinguished by hefty two-hand handles set at right angles to the blade. The pit saw is designed to rip a log lengthwise while being held at a nearly vertical angle. Two men operate it, one standing above the log, the other in a pit below it. Their alternate pulling, with sawdust showering down on the man below, cuts a smooth plank from the log. The expenditure of man-hours on such a tedious task seems almost incredible in the 1970s economy, but as we see elsewhere, the pioneer had more hours than dollars, and he needed the planks. The fact that the pit saw was widely used in Kentucky is attested to by the old pit saws that turn up occasionally at country auctions. A pit saw in good condition sold for $1.75 at a Western Kentucky auction in 1973. It would seem well worth that price to hang it up as a constant reminder that the good old days were not good in every respect.

Another nearly forgotten means of turning logs into boards without transporting them to a sawmill was the floating sawmill. This was a fully equipped sawmill installed on a floating barge and moved up and down navigable rivers to process logs on order. The owner of the logs would store them on the riverbank until the "sawboat" arrived, then have them sawn according to his own specifications. The floating sawmill made good sense in an area where river navigation was the best means of transportation, as was true of some areas along the course of the Barren River. An old-time resident there recalls that when his father got ready to build a new house, he piled suitable logs on the riverbank and sent word to Oliver's sawboat. When the sawboat arrived members of the family contributed labor to the milling.

Portable sawmills on the river had their counterparts in sawmills run by steam traction engines on land. Before internal combustion displaced steam-powered engines, a cumbersome, slow-moving steam tractor could propel itself to the mill site and set the great circular saw turning by means of a long belt running from flywheel to saw. Such a simple arrangement is nostalgically appealing in this ecology-conscious age. Chips and slabs from the milling operation were transferred to the engine for fuel, solving both disposal and energy-source problems simultaneously. The discharge of steam and sweet-smelling woodsmoke was not noxious, and noise pollution was minimal as the pleasant chuffing of a steam engine is hardly a whisper as compared with the exhaust racket of a gasoline or diesel engine.

Such mills were displaced long ago by more efficient mass production methods keyed to improved means for transporting logs. Not every steam traction engine found its way to the scrapyard, however. A farmer in Upton, Kentucky, was the subject of television feature journalism in 1973 when reporters discovered that he was still firing up the boiler of his old steamer and sawing logs occasionally, not as a romantic revival stunt, but as a commercial sideline.

It is usually easy to tell what kind of saw was used to cut unplaned lumber. The circular saw leaves arc-shaped tooth marks on the board surface. These are clearly visible on the board surfaces of the cotton gins illustrated on pages 52-53. If a board is quite old it may be worth examining for the straight marks left by the teeth of a pit saw. They will be at a slight angle away from vertical. The bandsaw of a modern mill cuts vertically, but it is so sharp and fast that it leaves no distinct mark on the face of the board.

73

7

EPILOGUE

IN THE LATE twentieth century a single substantial walnut tree may sell for more money than a typical pioneer farmer saw in a year's time. The pioneer's problem was the disposal of trees. It is a painful thought for a modern conservation-minded citizen who rarely or never sees a tree ten feet in diameter, but the values of people who needed corn more than they needed scenery dictated much of the destruction. As the population grew and commerce developed, inroads on Kentucky forests accelerated. Charcoal burning, keelboat and flatboat commerce downriver, and finally logging with essentially modern methods have effectively reduced the original timber stands. Income from a timber tract tided over many a hard-pressed farmer at a time when he could ill afford to be a conservationist even if he wanted to be one. Even so, Kentucky's forest resources have not been entirely destroyed.

Although one no longer finds large stands of virgin timber with trees up to ten feet in diameter in Kentucky, a pattern of conserving timber for sustained yield has gradually developed. Kentucky's mild climate favors many fast-growing species, so that periodic timber harvesting on land not suitable for profitable agriculture has settled into a pattern. The Department of Forestry reported in a recent year, for example, a harvest of eighty million board feet of poplar with a value of ten million dollars.

Meanwhile a strong conservation movement has resulted in the protection of some forest tracts. As these mature, at least some portions of the commonwealth will begin to resume the majesty of the primeval setting, providing enjoyment and renewal for the many instead of profit for the few.

Paralleling this forest conservation program in the space age is the popular do-it-yourself movement in which a new generation rediscovers the pleasure of working with hand tools. Some restore old wooden tools with loving care, then use them for their pleasurable associations. Some even go so far as to acquire an old log or hewn timber building, carefully number the pieces, and remove them one by one to a new site to be restored as a contemporary dwelling. Nostalgic romanticism seems to lie behind such an effort, but a well restored house with that much timber in its walls can appeal to the practical-minded too. It is sturdy and well insulated against noise and temperature change.

A massive bar share plow is a prized exhibit at the Kentucky Museum in Bowling Green. Like many other tools in the collection, this plow must tell its own story. Its

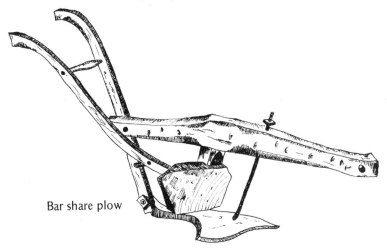

Bar share plow

maker is unknown. Whoever he was, he belonged to the era poised between the frontier and settled agricultural economy. His plow is a suitable symbol of the period, a symbol of cultivated fields displacing tracts of forest. The well wrought wooden body symbolizes a plentiful supply of raw materials and the skill to use it. The rough metal parts foreshadow the coming of foundries and factories.

The bar share plow and other wooden artifacts like it arouse the wonder and admiration of contemporary Kentuckians. Evidence of hard work, thrift, and ingenuity, these objects are tangible bits of history worthy of preservation and display.

Index to Illustrations

77